BAGGAGE CLAIM Workbook

Kimberly H. Miller Dr. Newton H. Miller II

newED publishing

TITLE: Baggage Claim 2nd Edition
By: Kimberly H. Miller and Dr. Newton H. Miller II
Cover: Ommyz World Creations
ISBN-13: 979-8-89292-507-5
Copyright 2023

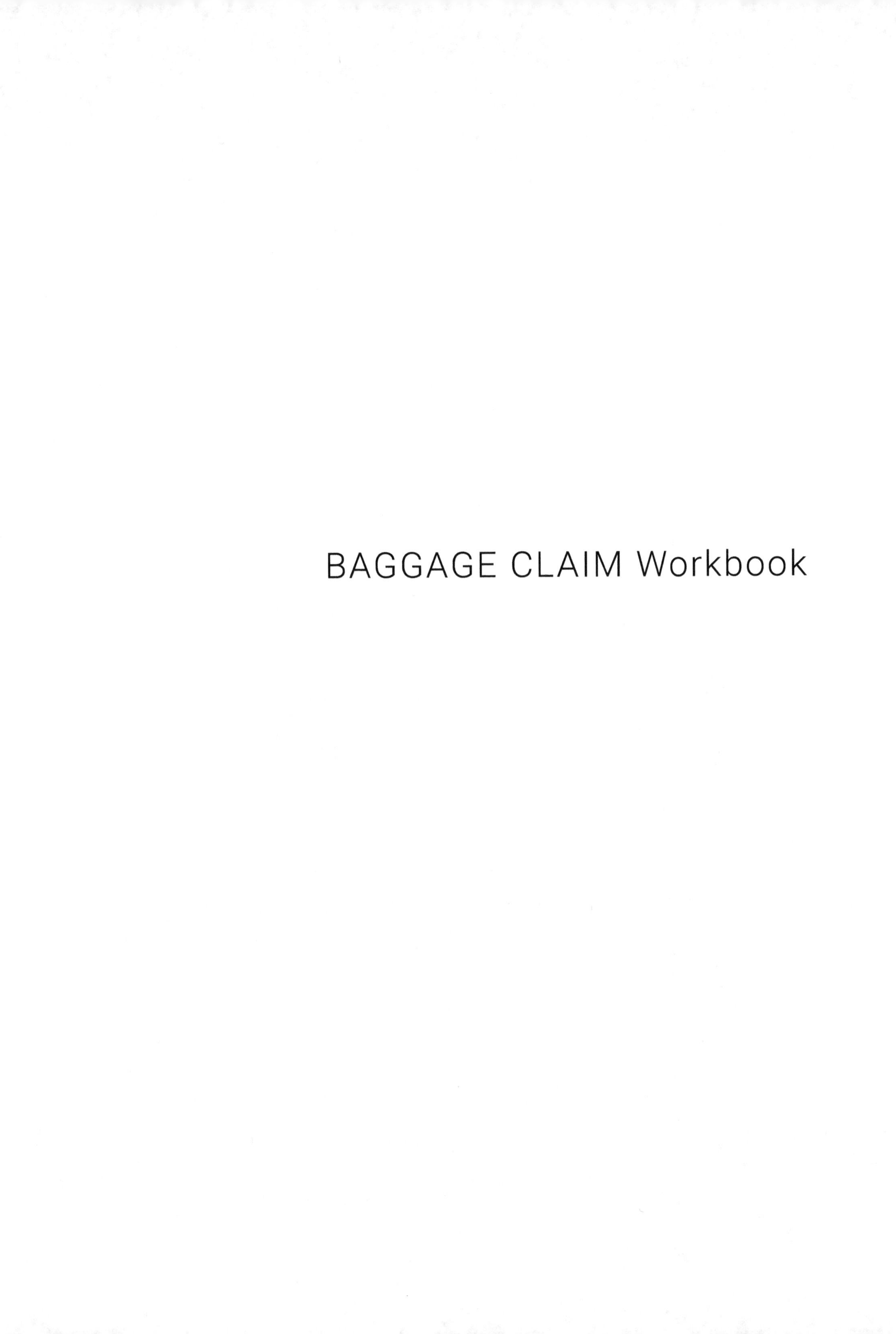

BAGGAGE CLAIM Workbook

CONTENTS

Introduction

Welcome to the workbook portion of the Baggage Claim experience. Congratulations on taking the first step towards building a stronger, more fulfilling marriage! Your decision to invest in this workbook is a testament to your commitment to growth and connection. This is a comprehensive guide designed to strengthen and invigorate your relationship. The ten activities in this workbook serve as a bank of interactive resources created to encourage open communication, understanding, and cooperation between partners. By delving into a series of exercises, discussions, and reflective tasks, this workbook aims to deepen the connection and mutual growth within your relationship. It offers a blend of practical exercises and insightful prompts to explore various facets of your partnership, encouraging teamwork, empathy, and fostering a stronger bond. Whether you're newlyweds seeking to build a solid foundation or a long-term couple looking to rekindle the flame, this workbook provides a roadmap for exploring, understanding, and enhancing the dynamics of your union.

The activities are comprehensive and progressive. Meaning they build upon each other. As you progress through each chapter of Baggage Claim a corresponding activity is introduced. The first five activities are designed for you to reflect on yourself and organize your thoughts around how you perceive your spouse. Then you will put your thoughts and feelings on paper as you prepare to share them with your spouse. You will learn the H.O.W. method, The Compromise Navigator, and conclude your experience with a post-test to compare with your pre-test.

The activities progress like this.

- Activity 1 is a pre-assessment in which participants will evaluate ten distinct components integral to their marital bond. This evaluation serves as a comparison point to the post-assessment conducted after engaging in the activities outlined in this workbook.
- Activity 2-4, Unpack your bags so you can communicate, and problem solve better in your marriage.
- By activity 5, – You will have done a deep dive into what's making you tick.
- Activity 6, you will journal what you've discovered about yourself and your wife.
- Activity 7, apply the H.O.W. method to train yourself to become more aware of ways to be open to and accept input to change.
- Activity 8 uses the 4R's to avoid getting stuck in the communication process before it progresses. This tool will help make sure that all your conversations in your marriage are a win-win.

- Activity 9 teaches us how to come to healthy compromises as we encounter times where opinions and stances differ.
- Activities 6, 7, and 8 are tools that you should adopt and use continuously for the duration of your marriage. However, they should not be attempted and integrated into your communication style until after considerable work on activities 1-5 has been completed.

Remember, every exercise within these pages is a step towards a more vibrant, resilient relationship. Embrace each activity with curiosity and enthusiasm, knowing that every effort you put in brings you closer to a deeper bond with your partner.

This journey might have its ups and downs, but it's in these moments of dedication and effort that real transformation happens. Celebrate your progress, no matter how small, and keep your eyes set on the beautiful future you're creating together.

Let this workbook be your guide, but let your love and determination be the fuel that propels you forward. Get ready for a journey filled with discovery, growth, and a newfound closeness that will enrich your lives in ways you never imagined.

You've got this!

Activity #1 - Pre-Assess your Marriage

To maintain a healthy marriage, you must commit to always *Provide for, Invest* in, and *Empower* one another. Although those ingredients may look and operate differently in each relationship, they are consistent ingredients in the batter of a happy and healthy marriage. The Rate Your Marriage activity is designed to help you analyze your relationship and evaluate each of its components so you can be more deliberate in creating a game plan to improve your love affair with your husband or wife.

We suggest you complete this copy of the Rate Your Marriage tool BEFORE reading Baggage Claim to pre-assess your own perception of each of the categories addressed in the tool. This tool is meant to be completed independently from your spouse, which means it is based on YOUR interpretation of each category, and YOUR perception of the score it deserves. Once you complete the tool on your own, schedule some time with your spouse to compare each other's assessments. Don't' be alarmed when your perception and your spouse's perceptions are different. More than likely, they will be. This is an opportunity to talk to one another, listen to one another, ask questions, and get a better understanding of each other's thoughts and feelings. Don't look now, but the work of building a better marriage has just begun.

Once you finish reading the whole book and working through the activities, you will complete the post version of the Assess Your Marriage Tool using the same procedure you used to complete the pre version. However, this time, include in the discussion of your assessment with your spouse a comparison between your pre and post version scores. To create a culture of continuous improvement in your marriage, complete and compare another post version of the tool at the three-month, six-month, and twelve-month marks. This will provide you with some data you can use to track how much your thinking has changed and how far your relationship has progressed. Most importantly, make sure you keep the conversation going.

Activity #1
Pre-Assess your Marriage

Rate each category on a scale of 1-10 *(10 the greatest and 1 the lowest). Provide a brief reason for the score.*

Category	Score	Reason
Goals / Drive/ Aspirations (Is there a sense that there is a common target or mission that you are accomplishing together?)		
Sex & Intimacy (How compatible are your sex drives, definitions of intimacy and priority levels when it comes to sex and intimacy?)		
Parenting/ Family Values (Consider whether your similarities and differences around family values and parenting complement each other or clash. Are they effective or damaging?)		
Dealing with Conflict (Consider how you resolve conflict in your marriage. Do you feel l you have a good understanding of how and when to address issue in your relationship?)		
Career & Money (How compatible are you in your style of handling money and prioritizing career?)		
Household Responsibilities (Are you happy with your household responsibilities?)		

Communication
(Do you feel like you try your best to understand each other's views, feelings, and opinions?)

Faith / Spirituality / Beliefs
(How spiritually compatible are you? Do you assist in each's spiritual growth?)

Friendship with Each Other
(Is your spouse your best friend?)

Managing External Friendships
(Are external relationships prioritized such that they are a help and not a hinderance to your marriage?)

Add the scores for each category to calculate your **Total Score**

Divide the Total Score by 10 to calculate the Average Score of Your Marriage. *(Total Score /10)*

Activity #2 - That's My Bag - Chapters 1 & 2

What are bags? Bags are personality traits or character issues that you take with you wherever you go. They show up and influence every one of your personal and professional relationships and interactions with others.

In this activity your task is to list a few personality traits or character issues about yourself (your bags), and your spouse. Hint, they are usually the things that people consistently mention that they notice about you.

** NOTE: Before you go any further, you will not be sharing your results for the next four activities with your spouse. This is a time of reflection, observation, and self-discipline. **

This is a simple task, but it may not be easy for everyone. We suggest that you consider the objective a day or two before actually listing your traits. This way you can be sure that what you have settled on is as accurate and aligned to you and your spouse as possible.

Objectives

Participants of this activity will:

• Identify their traits, strengths, weaknesses, and behavioral patterns in order to increase their awareness of the effect that things have on them and therefore how they are impacting others.

- Analyze their own personality traits to leverage them to assist with weaknesses and set goals for self-improvement.
- Outline their personality traits to determine how they may contribute to or extract from their ability to foster strong and healthy relationships.

Guiding Questions to ask yourself:

You do not have to use these questions. We just offered them as tools to jump start your thinking as you begin this activity. These questions can serve as a starting point for self-reflection on personality traits, aiding in the identification and understanding of various aspects of oneself. Engaging with these questions can offer valuable insights into personal characteristics and behavioral tendencies.

- **What are my natural tendencies in various situations?**

    This question helps in recognizing how you typically respond or behave in different scenarios. Are you more inclined to take charge, observe, assist, or withdraw? Understanding these tendencies can reveal underlying personality traits.

- **What are my strengths and weaknesses?**
Exploring personal strengths and weaknesses can offer insight into your personality traits. Identifying areas where you excel and where you might struggle often correlates with particular personality characteristics.
- **How do I interact with others?**
Assess your interpersonal interactions, communication style, and relationship dynamics. Are you naturally outgoing or reserved? Do you prefer working alone or in a team? Understanding how you engage with others reveals personality traits like extraversion, agreeableness, or introversion.
- **What brings me fulfillment and satisfaction?**

    Reflect on activities, interests, or situations that bring you joy, fulfillment, or satisfaction. Understanding what motivates and excites you can reveal your values, passions, and certain personality traits.

Activity #2
That's My Bag - Chapters 1 & 2
See the examples provided and then complete the chart.

Personality Traits or Character Issues

Self	Spouse
example #1 - Bossy	example #2 - Blunt

Activity #3 - Unpacking Your Bags - Chapters 3 & 4

Most of our lives, we have dealt with positive and negative comments about ourselves. For the most part, we seem to do okay with the comments, well at least until we have to look in the mirror and address the issues within ourselves.

In this activity, you will:

1. Examine the bags that you claimed in the "That's My Bag" worksheet from chapters 1 & 2 and
2. **List the behaviors that emerge because of those personality traits or character issues.**
3. **Also, find or describe a picture that depicts or represents that behavior.**
4. Repeat the same steps (1-3) on the second chart, but only for the baggage you identified for your spouse.

Keep in mind that these behaviors are a direct result of the bags you and your spouse are carrying. If you do this activity correctly, you will have two separate charts (*His and Hers)* displaying personality traits and behaviors for you on one chart and for your spouse on another.

Remember, you will not share the results of either chart with your spouse until we complete activity #5.

Please allow us to offer some friendly Advice. To maximize the value of this intrusive self-reflective exercise, three key steps are essential. First, approach the exercise with an open and honest mindset. This means embracing vulnerability and being willing to confront uncomfortable truths about oneself. Second, it is crucial to set aside dedicated time and space for introspection. Creating an environment that fosters focus and introspection without distractions allows for a deeper exploration of thoughts and emotions. Lastly, aim to apply the insights gained from this self-reflective exercise into your daily life. This involves actively incorporating newfound awareness into actions, decision-making, and interactions, enabling personal growth and positive change. Embracing openness, dedicating time, and implementing learned insights are pivotal in maximizing the value you will gain from this and any other intrusive self-reflective exercise.

Objectives
Participants of this activity will:

- Recognize connections between traits and behaviors to gain insight into why certain actions or reactions occur in specific situations.
- Analyze how traits manifest into actions or responses to potentially alter repetitive behaviors that may be hindering personal growth or relationships.
- Identify strengths and behaviors that might be causing difficulties to set goals towards self-improvement and growth.
- Contemplate strategies to leverage positive traits and transform negative behaviors for better self-control and emotional intelligence.

Guiding Questions to ask yourself:
Once again, you do not have to use these questions. They are provided as you get started determining the behaviors that emerge as a result of your personality traits.

They provide a structured approach to listing personality traits and understanding how they translate into behaviors. They guide the introspective process, allowing for a deeper understanding of oneself and potential areas for personal development.

- **What are my dominant personality traits and how do they manifest in my behavior?**
  Start by identifying the primary personality traits you believe you possess. Then, explore how these traits are expressed in your behaviors and actions in different situations. For instance, if you consider yourself conscientious, how does this reflect in your organizational skills or attention to detail?
- **In what situations do specific behaviors tend to emerge based on my traits?**
  Explore the contexts or situations in which certain behaviors linked to your traits tend to surface. Recognizing the triggers or environments where these behaviors become prominent provides insight into how your traits interact with various circumstances.

- **How do these behaviors impact my interactions and relationships with others?**
Reflect on how your behaviors, influenced by your traits, affect your relationships and interactions. Consider whether certain behaviors facilitate positive connections or if they cause challenges in your interactions with others.
- **Can I identify areas for personal development or improvement based on these trait-behavior connections?**

Analyze whether there are behaviors resulting from specific traits that may require improvement or modification. Identifying areas for personal growth allows you to set goals for enhancing positive behaviors or altering behaviors that might hinder personal or professional development.

Activity #3
Unpacking Your Bags - Chapters 3 & 4
<u>*HERS CHART*</u>
View the examples provided and then complete the chart.

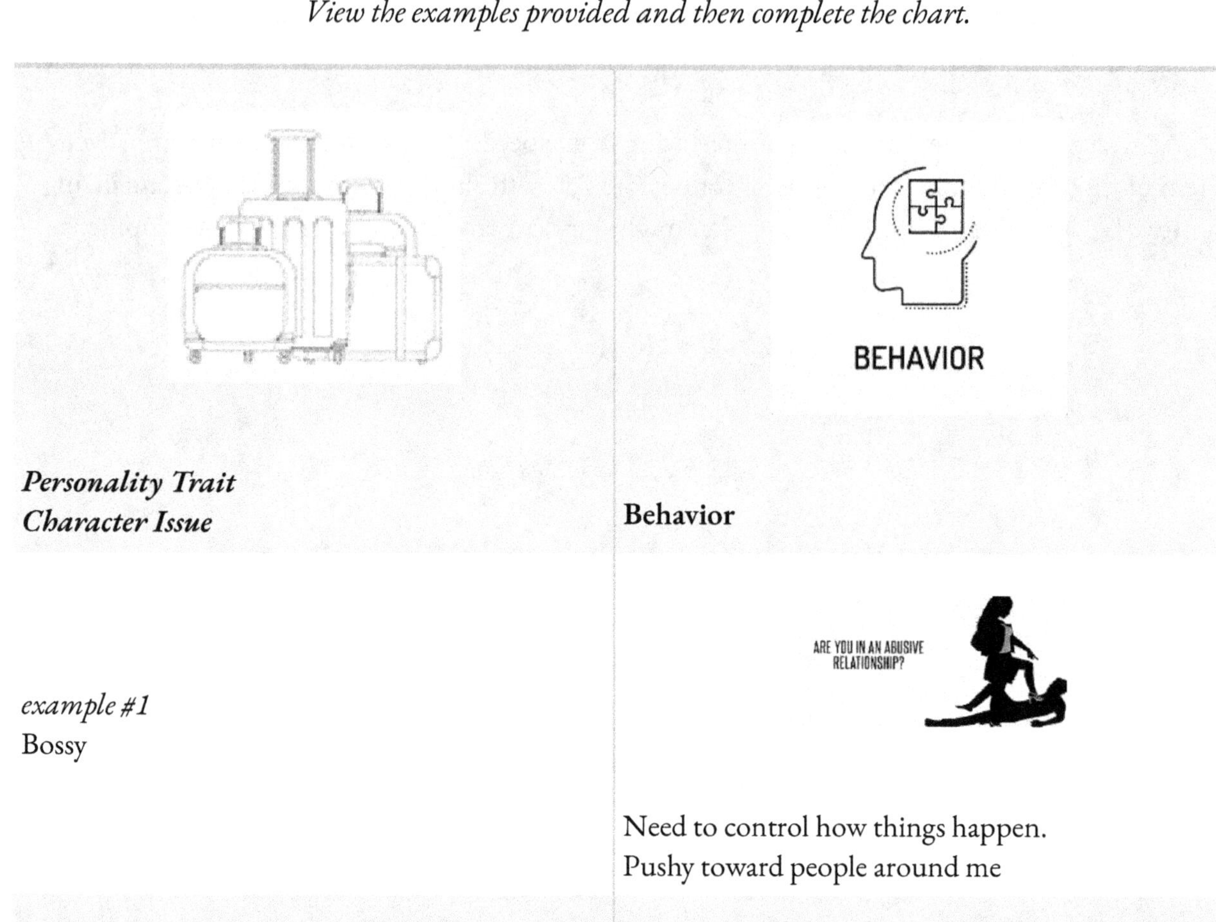

Personality Trait Character Issue	**Behavior**
example #1 Bossy	Need to control how things happen. Pushy toward people around me
example #2 Direct Blunt	Inconsiderate of the feelings of others Unfiltered choice of words

Behaviors

1.

2.

Behaviors

1.

2.

Behaviors

1.

2.

Activity #3
Unpacking Your Bags - Chapters 3 & 4
<u>*HIS CHART*</u>
View the examples provided and then complete the chart.

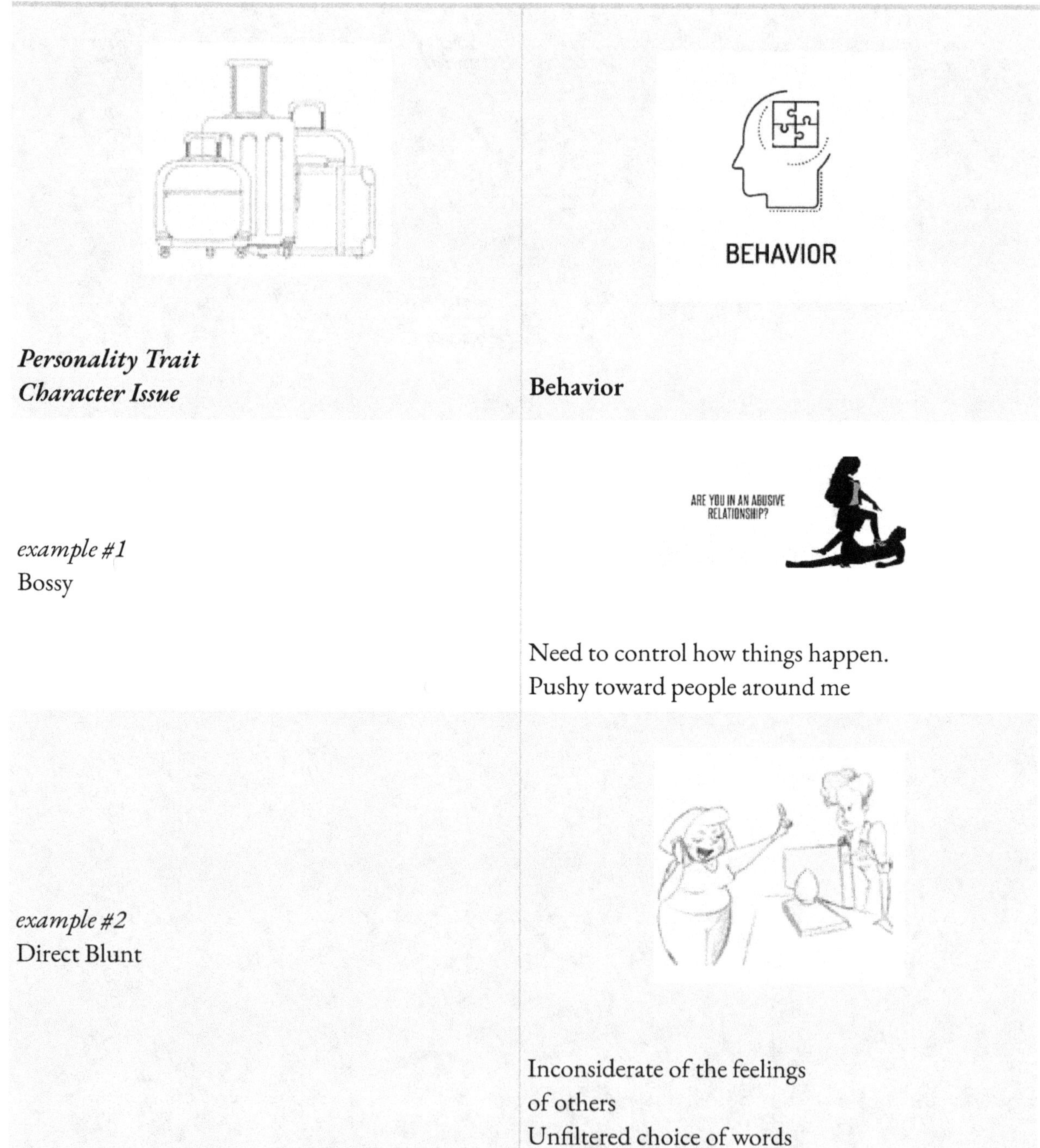

Personality Trait *Character Issue*	**Behavior**
example #1 Bossy	Need to control how things happen. Pushy toward people around me
example #2 Direct Blunt	Inconsiderate of the feelings of others Unfiltered choice of words

Behaviors

1.

2.

Behaviors

1.

2.

Behaviors

1.

2.

Activity #4 - Blame it on the Bags – Chapters 5 & 6

Accepting responsibility for our actions is quite humbling and honestly sometimes a little embarrassing. It is easy to project and push the blame for our actions onto those who may have identified or exposed the behaviors within us.

Identifying, accepting, and being accountable for our own actions can be an arduous yet profoundly positive process. It demands an elevated level of introspection and self-awareness that often requires us to confront uncomfortable truths about ourselves. Acknowledging our actions, especially when they have caused harm or have been less than admirable, can be challenging and emotionally taxing.

However, this process is vital for personal growth and fostering healthier relationships. Embracing accountability empowers us to learn from our mistakes, make amends, and take proactive steps toward positive change. It is a challenging journey, but one that leads to a deeper understanding of ourselves, encourages self-improvement, and cultivates a sense of responsibility for our impact on the world around us. Ultimately, by accepting and being accountable for our actions, we pave the way for personal evolution and more meaningful connections with others.

For this activity, you will, without judgment, accept and address your actions, so you can begin to create a different approach to walk towards change. Be thorough but give yourself a break. We are smack dab in the middle of our journey and although it is often uncomfortable, self-work is the best work!

Also, you will be filling out a chart uncovering what you perceive your spouse's baggage makes them do. Although you will be truthful and thorough in communicating your perceptions of your spouse, record them with grace. Be considerate, this is your spouse, the love of your life that you are writing about. Your words should be seasoned with grace and compassion just as you want the perceptions of others to be served to you.

In this activity, you will:

1. Examine the bags that you claimed in the "That's My Bag" worksheet from chapters 1 & 2 and

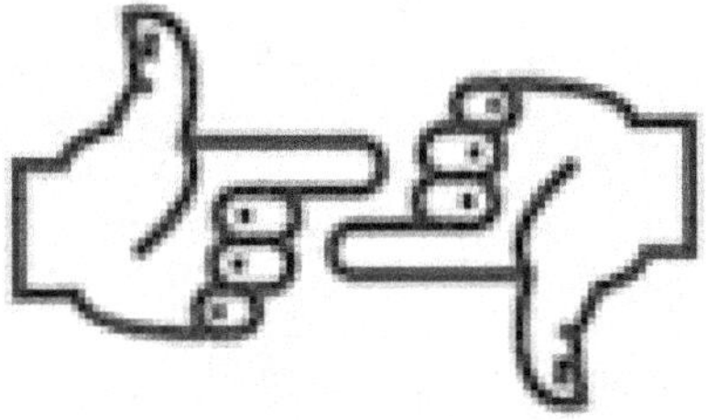

2.

List the behaviors and provide or describe the pictures that emerge because of those personality traits or character issues.
3. **Describe how those behaviors manifest (what do they look like or make you do) when relating with others.**
4. Repeat the same steps (1-3) on the second chart, but only for the baggage you identified for your spouse.

Keep in mind that what you enter on this chart is a direct result of the bags you and your spouse are carrying. If you do this activity correctly, you will have two separate charts (*His and Hers*) displaying personality traits and behaviors for you on one chart and for your spouse on another.

Remember, you will not share the results of either chart with your spouse until we complete activity #5.

Objectives

Participants of this activity will:

- Acknowledge and take ownership of one's behaviors linked to specific personality traits.
- Analyze how one's traits influence behaviors that might not align with personal values or goals.
- Establish accountability for behaviors to understand how they influence actions, reactions, and decisions in various situations.
- Address potential areas for improvement in communication or behavior to foster healthier and more constructive relationships.

Guiding Questions to ask yourself:

Some of you may need jump starter questions to help you complete this activity and some of you will not. Just to be safe, we provided you with these guiding questions to provide a structured approach that might help you reflect on behaviors associated with identifying personality traits and behaviors for which we need to take accountability.

- **How do my identified personality traits influence my behaviors in various situations?**

    Begin by examining the ways in which your identified personality traits affect your behaviors. Reflect on specific instances or scenarios where these traits tend to influence your actions, reactions, and decision-making processes.

- **In what ways have these behaviors impacted me and others?**
Reflect on the consequences of your behaviors associated with these traits. Consider how these actions might have affected your own well-being and the well-being of those around you, whether positively or negatively.

- **What changes can I make to align my behaviors with my desired values and goals?**
Explore how you can take proactive steps to modify or adjust behaviors to better align with your personal values and long-term objectives. Consider strategies for managing or altering these behaviors in a way that fosters positive outcomes.

- **How can I communicate and take responsibility for my actions in a constructive manner?**

    Consider how to communicate accountability for these behaviors. Reflect on ways to take responsibility and communicate this to oneself and, where necessary, to others, in a constructive and growth-oriented manner, promoting understanding and positive change.

Activity #4
Blame it on the Bags – Chapters 5 & 6
HERS CHART

See the examples provided and then complete the chart.

Personality Trait	BEHAVIOR	*Results*
Character Issue	**Behavior**	*(What the bags make me do)*
example #1 Blunt	Inconsiderate of the feelings of others Unfiltered choice of words	I usually don't think about my words before I say them. My responses are typically emotional reactions that can be offensive to others.
example #2 Bossy	Need to control how things happen. Pushy toward people around me	I'm impatient and used to being in charge, which prompts me to use commanding prompts to get things done when I want and how I want. Unfortunately, people in contact with me find this behavior to be demanding and inconsiderate.

Behaviors

1.

2.

Behaviors

1.

2.

Behaviors

1.

2.

Activity #4
Blame it on the Bags – Chapters 5 & 6
<u>HIS CHART</u>

See the examples provided and then complete the chart.

Personality Trait		*Results*
	BEHAVIOR	*(What the bags make me do)*
Character Issue	**Behavior**	
	Inconsiderate of the feelings of others Unfiltered choice of words	
example #1 Blunt		I usually don't think about my words before I say them. My responses are typically emotional reactions that can be offensive to others.
example #2 Bossy	Need to control how things happen. Pushy toward people around me	I'm impatient and used to being in charge, which prompts me to use commanding prompts to get things done when I want and how I want. Unfortunately, people in contact with me find this behavior to be demanding and inconsiderate.
	Behaviors 1. 2.	

	Behaviors 1. 2.	
	Behaviors 1. 2.	

Activity #5 - The Gift in My Bag - Chapter 7 & 8

Stubbornness can manifest as determination and persistence, essential qualities for achieving long-term goals. Impulsiveness might reflect a spontaneous and adventurous spirit, adding excitement and innovation to life. Sensitivity can be a marker of empathy and deep emotional understanding, facilitating more profound connections with others.

Recognizing and harnessing these hidden gifts within traits perceived as negative not only fosters self-acceptance but also enables individuals to leverage their unique strengths for personal development, building resilience, and nurturing healthier relationships. Embracing these hidden positives within seemingly negative traits allows for a more holistic and appreciative understanding of oneself and ability to nurture meaningful relationships with others.

This activity challenges you to look at what you previously viewed as negative personality traits, character issues, and behaviors, and with a small cognitive shift and a little positive thinking, look for the benefits in them. Then you will identify how you can accept the positivity of those traits, integrate them into your everyday actions such that you capitalize on their power and influence in ways that are productive to your relationship.

In this activity:

1. Examine the bags that you claimed in the "That's My Bag" worksheet from chapters 1 & 2 and
2. List the behaviors and provide or describe the pictures that emerge because of those personality traits or character issues.
3. **Shift that negative trait and rename it as a positive asset or a gift to others.**
4. **Describe the behaviors of the traits that you have just renamed, only from a positive perspective.**
5. Repeat the same steps (1-3) on the second chart, but only for how you perceive your spouse from a positive perspective.

Objectives

Participants of this activity will:

- Identify positive aspects or strengths that lie within traits often labeled as negative.
- Develop a more accepting and appreciative attitude of self-esteem and a healthier self-image.
- Outline positive attributes and harness them as strengths to stimulate self-improvement and development. Thus, fostering a more holistic and balanced personality.
- Utilize the positive aspects of traits once deemed to be negative in order to improve relationships.

Guiding Questions to ask yourself:

You may not use these questions at all...and that's perfectly fine. They are provided as you get started determining the behaviors that emerge as a result of your personality traits.

They are meant to serve as a framework for introspection, allowing individuals to explore perceived negative traits and behaviors, identify hidden strengths within them, and develop strategies for utilizing these strengths for personal development and improved interactions.

- **What are the specific traits or behaviors I or others perceive as negative?**
  Start by identifying the traits or behaviors you or others might view as negative. This might include traits like impatience, introversion, or perfectionism, or behaviors such as avoidance or overthinking.
- **How might these perceived negative traits have benefited me in certain situations?**
  Explore past experiences and situations in which these traits or behaviors, usually labeled as negative, might have offered advantages, or contributed positively. For instance, has perfectionism ever led to outstanding attention to detail or high-quality work?
- **What strengths or positive attributes could be associated with these negative traits or behaviors?**
  Investigate the positive aspects or strengths hidden within these supposedly negative traits. For instance, how might impatience manifest as decisiveness or a drive for efficiency? How might introversion offer deeper introspection or keen observation skills?
- **How can I leverage these hidden gifts to improve my life or relationships?**

Reflect on how to use the discovered strengths associated with these negative traits to enhance your life and interactions. Consider how to harness these hidden gifts to foster personal growth, improve relationships, and navigate various situations more effectively.

Activity #5
The Gift in My Bag - Chapter 7 & 8
HER CHART

See the example provided and then complete the chart.

Personality Trait Character Issue	*Behavior*	**Shift to a Positive Perspective**	**What the New Actions Look Like**
example #1 *Bossy*	*Controlling & Pushy*	*Leader*	*I am confident and organized when approaching a task. I usually know exactly what I need to ask from others to do in order to help accomplish the task that I envision.*

Activity #5
The Gift in My Bag - Chapter 7 & 8
<u>*HIS CHART*</u>
See the example provided and then complete the chart.

Personality Trait Character Issue	*Behavior*	**Shift to a Positive Perspective**	**What the New Actions Look Like**
example #1 *Bossy*	*Controlling & Pushy*	*Leader*	*I am confident and organized when approaching a task. I usually know exactly what I need to ask from others to do in order to help accomplish the task that I envision.*

6

Activity #6 - Debrief – How These Bags Make Me Feel

This activity begins with you handing over the charts that you filled out about your spouse from activity #1-5 to them. Don't provide any explanation, just hand them over and walk away. The second part of activity #6 is a writing activity or debrief, where we explore the intricate landscape of our self-reflection, delving into the discovery of our negative traits and behaviors.

It's a unique journey that involves scrutinizing not just our own perceptions but also the perceptions of those around us. In this exercise we'll navigate the emotions surfaced by the acknowledgment of these negative aspects—traits and behaviors that might have been hidden, unrecognized, or unacknowledged. Through this process, we aim to untangle the complex interplay between how we perceive ourselves and how others view us concerning these less favorable traits and behaviors.

This debrief will allow for a deeper exploration of the feelings and insights that emerged from this self-reflective journey, opening doors to understanding, acceptance, and the potential for personal growth.

This activity is an especially important step in our journey together for two reasons. This is the first time that we are pausing to reflect on everything we have done since the pre-assessment in activity #1. Pausing to consider your traits, behaviors, and both negative and positive actions can bring all kinds of thoughts and emotions to the surface. This is your opportunity to chew on, swallow and digest everything so you can stay open-minded and able to communicate with your spouse about what has been discovered and revealed.

Secondly, after you complete your writing piece, you will talk with your spouse to share your feelings about your debrief. This is a powerful experience. You get to hear how they perceive you, and you get to tell them how you perceive yourself. That exercise will unlock a new dimension of support, encouragement, and understanding for one another that will catapult your relationship into higher heights and deeper depths.

At this point, your mind is probably all over the place. So, we provided a template to help organize your thoughts and guide your writing. By no means do you have to use this template to maximize the impact of this activity. As long as you address how you feel about the discoveries and feedback you have received thus far, identify the truth that you are accepting, and provide some sort of affirmation that speaks to the solutions or what you will do to reverse the negative or abrasive perceptions that your spouse has shared with you, you will gain great returns from this exercise..

In this activity:

1. Review the charts in which your spouse shares their perceptions of you and consider what you discovered about yourself in activities #1-5 as well.
2. Using the template provided, or your own format, write a debrief sharing how all these bags make you feel.
3. Wait a day or two to allow things to marinate and then sit down to talk with your spouse about what you wrote.
4. Describe the behaviors of the traits that you have just renamed, only from a positive perspective.
5. End your conversation with two affirmations.
   1. A statement of what you are going to do to multiply the positive perceptions and experiences that your spouse has with you.
   2. Remind your spouse how much you love them by telling them exactly that before you conclude this activity.

Objectives

Participants of this activity will:

- Synthesize what one discovered about themselves alongside their spouse's observations to improve communication and foster healthier relationship dynamics.
- Process the information shared by one's spouse to gain a deeper understanding of oneself by reflecting on personal insights and observations.
- Identify areas for personal growth that might positively impact their relationship.
- Develop improved empathy and greater understanding for each other's perspectives within the relationship.

Activity #6
Debrief – How These Bags Make Me Feel

As you do your written debrief you are welcome to use our four-square template to process your thoughts and responses. Since this activity is so important to the "Baggage" method, for convenience and clarity, we have provided video explanations to assist you as you complete this written debrief.

Example Chart

1. **Feelings** (How do I feel after reviewing all of these reflections?) • I'm angry because... • How dare they say that about me? • I don't feel like talking right now. • I need to create some alone time while I process.	1. **Questions** (Arguments against the perceptions of my behaviors) • Don't they know that everything I've done has been to help? • Why would they say that? I always support them. • Why is it that I'm the only one who remembers what I've done to make things work? • Wow, do they even appreciate me?
1. **Justifications/Responses** (The reasons I've done the things that I've done.) • The reason I'm upset is because... • I spend time alone because... • I've done so much, and no one seems to appreciate it, so I celebrate myself.	1. **Truth/Acceptance** (The truth about my behaviors that I am willing to accept.) • Maybe I can slow down and be more intentional about considering the perspective of others before drawing conclusions.

Activity #6 - Debrief – How These Bags Make Me Feel

1. **Feelings** (How do I feel after reviewing all of these reflections?)

1. **Questions** (Arguments against the perceptions of my behaviors)

1. **Justifications/Responses** (The reasons I've done the things that I've done.)

1. **Truth/Acceptance** (The truth about my behaviors that I am willing to accept.)

7

Activity #7 - Just Pick One - Chapter 9

In this action planning activity, we'll concentrate on the deliberate development of a specific trait and its associated behavior. The purpose is to create a roadmap for personal growth by focusing on one identified trait or behavior that holds potential for improvement. By narrowing our attention to a single trait, we aim to harness our efforts effectively, enabling a more targeted and intentional approach towards self-improvement. Through this activity, we'll outline a structured plan, including actionable steps and strategies tailored to enhance this particular trait or behavior, fostering positive change and personal development.

This activity is titled "Just Pick One" because you will focus on one of the traits and behaviors that you and your spouse identified as problematic as you were completing activities 1-5. The caveat is that you will use the H.O.W. method to derive an action plan to address it. H.O.W. is a step-by-step method that you can apply to identify issues, gather information, and make changes. It requires three simple things: 1) You must get brutally **honest** about a shortcoming or area of need, 2) You must be **open** to receiving feedback, constructive criticism, and advice aimed at ways you can make changes to that identified area, and 3) Be **willing** to do whatever is necessary tom make adjustments toward positive change.

This is the first activity where you and your spouse will build something together. It is during this process that you will become vulnerable to your spouse. This process can be a little difficult and uncomfortable but remember the previous work that you have completed and stay on the course. You are halfway there!

In this activity:

1.

Reflect on the debrief conversation you had with your spouse and choose one trait or behavior that you want to focus on.

2. **Discuss with your spouse to decide exactly what it is about that trait that you want to get honest about and present that sentence in the "Honest" column in your chart.**

3. **Repeat step two except your focus is on what you will be open to receive and who you will be open to receive it from.**

4. **As was done in step one and two, speak with your spouse to decide and state what you will be willing to do in order to exact change in your life.**

Please keep in mind that you are only picking one thing to get honest about. We can't change everything at once. This is an opportunity to sort through what's needed most to enhance communications. It is suggested that you and your spouse record your one thing on separate charts. This way you can return to this chart and use a new row to record the next trait or behavior that you wish to address.

Objectives
Participants of this activity will:

- Concentrate on the enhancement of a specific trait and its associated behavior to outline a clear direction for personal growth.
- Outline specific, actionable steps and strategies to improve an identified trait and behavior.
- Adopt a deeper self-awareness and accountability.
- Create a plan with clear goals and milestones to track and measure progress in developing a targeted trait and behavior.

Guiding Questions to ask yourself:
These guiding questions can help you align your thoughts to encourage a mindset of transparency and receptiveness for personal development. The idea is to facilitate a more sincere and effective self-reflective action planning activity.

We have included these guiding questions to serve as a foundation for structuring an action plan to develop a specific trait and behavior. Employing the "honest, open, and willing" approach in a self-reflective action planning activity involves being candid, receptive, and motivated to foster personal development. Here are four guiding questions aligned with this approach:

1. **Am I being completely honest about the current state of this trait and behavior?**
   - Start by evaluating your honest perception of the current status of the identified trait and behavior. Assess whether you're open and transparent with yourself regarding its impact and how it is manifested in your actions.
2. **Am I open to feedback and suggestions for improving this trait and behavior?**
   - Assess your willingness to receive feedback or guidance from others about the identified trait and behavior. Consider if you're open-minded and receptive to alternative perspectives or suggestions for improvement.
3. **What specific steps am I willing to take to enhance this trait and behavior?**
   - Reflect on your willingness and motivation to take specific steps to develop the trait and behavior. Assess your commitment to implementing changes or adopting new approaches for improvement.
4. **How can I maintain an open and receptive mindset throughout this development process?**
   - Consider strategies to sustain an open and willing attitude throughout the action planning and development process. Reflect on how to remain receptive to feedback, open to change, and willing to adapt to facilitate meaningful growth.

Activity #7
Just Pick One - Chapter 9
See the example provided and then complete one row of the chart. After working on the first area
for 4 to 6 weeks. Repeat the process for a second item on a new row. Make this a regular part of your
self-reflection and development process.

Honest

Example #1
I don't like to seem like I'm
unintelligent, or I don't know how
to do things.

Open

I will be open to begin receiving
constructive criticism from those
closest to me.

Willing

I am willing to ask for help from
those closest to me and implement
their suggestions.

8

Activity #8 - The 4R's – Chapter 10

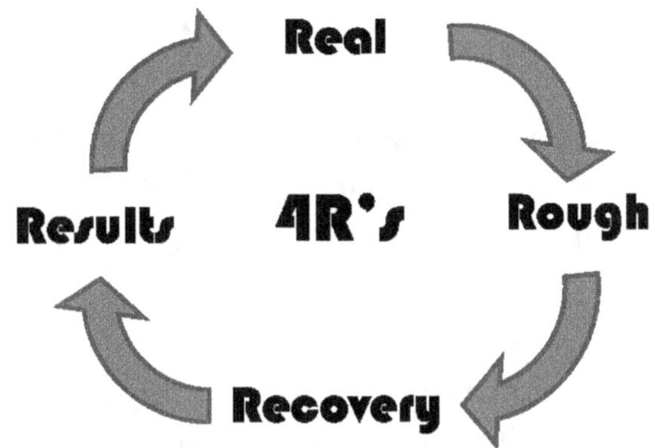

In this activity, you will analyze an actual tough conversation that you have had with your spouse in order to become aware of its four stages. AFTER your difficult conversation, when the two of you have come to a point where you can talk to and hear each other, this tool/activity will be tremendously helpful. You will sit together and re-hash the conversation, not to try to re-live the trauma, but to find where the conversation transitioned through each of the four phases of the 4R's.

The 4R's activity will help you be more aware of the shifts in the lifecycle of a difficult conversation. It will help you become more emotionally intelligent such that you are aware of your reactions and responses during the conversation and, more importantly, how they are affecting your spouse.

Objectives

Participants of this activity will:

- Recognize and acknowledge their genuine emotions and reactions during challenging conversations.
- Explore the difficulties faced, the conflicts encountered, and the discomfort experienced during difficult conversations, providing an opportunity for introspection, and understanding.

- Reflect on how to recover from the rough patches, learn from the experience, and identify strategies for personal development and improved communication in future interactions.
- Derive results from the self-reflective process, such as gaining insights, fostering understanding, and implementing changes that lead to improved communication, relationships, and personal development.

Guiding Questions to ask yourself:

These guiding questions can help you maximize the effectiveness of the 4R process. Although you do not have to use them, if you get stuck, it is our hope that they will help aim your thoughts to prompt introspection, foster self-awareness, and guide you through the 4R activity as you become more aware of navigating the transitions in rough conversations. Thus, leading to personal growth and improved communication skills.

Real:

What emotions did I genuinely experience during this challenging conversation?

Encourage an exploration of authentic emotions felt during the conversation. This question helps individuals identify and acknowledge their real feelings, fostering emotional awareness.

Rough:

What specific challenges or conflicts emerged during this conversation?

Prompt reflection on the difficulties encountered, conflicts faced, or areas of discomfort experienced. Encourage a deeper exploration of the rough patches and obstacles encountered in the conversation.

Recovery:

How can I learn and grow from this experience to recover and improve for future conversations?

Guide individuals to reflect on the lessons learned from the challenges faced. Encourage them to identify strategies for personal growth, recovery from difficult situations, and improvements in communication.

Results:

What constructive insights or changes can I derive from this experience to enhance future interactions?

Encourage a focus on deriving constructive outcomes from the conversation. Guide individuals to reflect on actionable insights gained and how these can be applied to facilitate better communication and positive outcomes in future interactions.

Activity #8
The 4R's – Chapter 10
Review the examples provided and then complete the chart.

PHASE	TRANSITION LANGUAGE	YOUR REACTIONS	YOUR SPOUSE'S REACTIONS
example *REAL*	*"You act like you care about the kids and the people at your job more than me. I need attention and affection too."*	***Responded to defend and explain.*** *"They are just kids; they need my attention. Isn't that what fathers are supposed to do? What are you saying… that's my job? That job is how I pay the bills, and I need to be available when they call and be nice and cordial when they do."*	***Hurt, deflated, and rejected. Steps into fight or flight mode.*** *She informs me that what I just said confirms her statement and begins to question why she even needs to be here at all.*
REAL			

example *ROUGH*	*"I can't believe this. Why are you making something out of nothing?"*	**Responded to defend and justify.** *"I'm trying to climb in my career and increase my income so we can live a better life. I put up with stuff all day, come home and get this from you. This feels self-centered, inconsiderate, and immature... Give me a break!"*	**Offended and now in full fight or flight mode.** *"No need for you to call me names. I'm just telling you how I feel and what I want from you. I should be the most important thing in your life besides God."*
ROUGH			
example *RECOVERY*	*"You are important, I never said that you weren't"*	**Hearing spouse's feelings and needs. Tries to find the words through the emotions to respond.** *"It's just that there is a lot of pressure on me to perform in every arena in my life. Maybe I need to re-evaluate some of my priorities."*	**Recognizing how the weight of the expectations on the spouse could result in their recent behaviors, understanding, and support enter the picture.** *"I can see there's a lot on you, but we are a team. How can I be there for you so you can be there for me?"*

RECOVERY

example
RESULTS

"You're right, we're on the same team. We win and lose together."

Accepts that seeking a solution is more important than making a point.
"Maybe I can revisit my schedule and block time for us to enjoy each other. I can also keep work at work and focus on home while I'm home."

Steps into solution mode and finds ways that everyone's needs can be met.
"If you let me know when you need time at home for work, I can keep everyone away so you can finish quicker. How about we set a date night, and I can plan the first few. Maybe we should have a 20-minute time slot each day where we debrief from our jobs with one another. This way we can be aware of how to support each other better."

RESULTS

9

Activity #9 - Keys and Compromise Tool – Chapter 11

In this activity we introduce the Keys and Compromise Tool, an innovative activity designed to navigate couples through the intricate process of arriving at compromises using the seven essential keys. This structured approach employs the "Compromise Navigator," a valuable tool crafted to assist couples in finding common ground. The seven keys serve as guiding principles, fostering understanding, communication, and collaboration within relationships. By utilizing this tool, couples can delve into the intricate aspects of compromise, focusing on mutual respect, communication, and the balance between individual needs and shared goals. The Keys and Compromise Tool empowers couples to navigate complexities, fostering a more harmonious and understanding relationship dynamic.

The Keys and Compromise tool combines the 7 keys to Compromise, and the Compromise Navigator into a powerful at-a-glance system. This tool can be used individually or together before, during, or after a conversation.

For this activity you will:

1. Identify and agree on a topic upon which you and your spouse each have a different opinion. (i.e., Where to vacation, What home improvement project should be next, how to raise children in a blended family...etc.)
2. Review the 7 Keys to compromise and agree upon them as the ground rules for your discourse.
3. Then use the steps of the navigator that apply to your particular conversation as a guide to keep the discussion productive as it progresses toward a positive resolve.
4. When you first start using Keys and Compromise Tool, don't be afraid to leave it out on the table and deliberately refer to it as you and your spouse talk.
5. In essence, let the tool function as a mediator that reminds you of how to keep your conversation focused, healthy, and productive.

Objectives

Participants of this activity will:

- Learn and practice effective communication strategies that foster understanding, active listening, and mutual respect, contributing to healthier dialogue and resolution.
- Navigate disagreements more effectively, leading to mutually acceptable resolutions.
- Deepen their connection, build trust, and demonstrate a willingness to work collaboratively towards mutually beneficial outcomes.
- Develop the skills necessary for collaborative decision-making, acknowledging each other's perspectives and needs in reaching compromises.

Guiding Questions to ask yourself:

If needed, these guiding questions will help you use the Keys and Compromise Tool activity to facilitate constructive discussions, encourage empathy and understanding, and guide you through the process of arriving at compromises using the seven keys, ultimately leading to mutually beneficial resolutions.

1. **What are our individual needs and priorities in this situation?**
   ◦ Encourage each partner to express their individual needs and priorities openly. This question initiates the process by establishing a clear understanding of each person's perspectives and desires.
2. **How can we actively listen and acknowledge each other's viewpoints?**
   ◦ Foster a culture of active listening and mutual respect by encouraging partners to listen attentively to each other's viewpoints. This question emphasizes the importance of acknowledging and validating each other's perspectives.
3. **What compromises or concessions are we willing to make to find a solution?**

- Guide couples to explore potential compromises or concessions they are willing to make to reach a resolution. This question encourages the partners to consider alternatives that accommodate both sets of needs and priorities.

4. **How can we use the 7 Keys to guide our discussion and decision-making?**
   - Encourage the utilization of the seven keys as a guiding framework for the discussion. This question prompts couples to apply these keys—such as empathy, flexibility, and patience—in their communication and decision-making process to arrive at a mutually agreeable compromise.

Activity #9
Keys and Compromise Tool

7 Keys to Compromise

- *Don't always try to be right*
- *Let things go*
- *Re-think your desired outcomes*
- *Show that you are willing to change*

- *Share your thoughts, feelings, and beliefs*
- *Appreciate your partner's efforts*
- *Remain open to doing it all again*

Compromise Navigator

Step 1	Review the Seven Keys to Compromise and ask yourself and your spouse these supporting questions: • Which of the seven keys will be most challenging? • What can we do to ensure that we adhere to the seven keys?
Step 2	Verbally agree that you will do your absolute best to apply the Seven Keys of Compromise before you begin your discussion.
Step 3	Choose who will speak first and let them finish expressing their thoughts, feelings, and position BEFORE responding.
Step 4	Respond to what your partner has just said not to present a rebuttal, but to get your thoughts, feelings, and beliefs on the table.
Step 5	Offer solutions to the situation and tell why you believe the solution you're offering is a good one.
Step 6	Both partners must agree to the plan and verbally restate it to each other to ensure that they are on the same page and agreeing to the same thing.
Step 7	Tell your spouse how much you appreciate their willingness to "come – to – a – promise" with you.

10

Activity #10 - Post – Assess Your Marriage – Chapter 12

To maintain a healthy marriage, you must commit to always *Provide for, Invest* in, and *Empower* one another. Although those ingredients may look and operate differently in each relationship, they are consistent in the batter of a happy and healthy marriage.

Welcome to the post-assessment phase, a crucial step in your journey toward enhancing your marriage relationship. In this assessment, participants will evaluate ten distinct components integral to their marital bond. This evaluation serves as a comparison point to the pre-assessment conducted before engaging in the activities outlined in this workbook. By comparing the pre-assessment and this post-assessment, participants gain insights into their progress, allowing them to gauge the impact of the workbook activities on their relationship. This post-assessment aims to measure growth, changes, and areas of improvement, offering a comprehensive view of the strides made and the evolution of various facets within your marriage.

The Assess Your Marriage activity is designed to help you analyze your relationship and evaluate each of its components so you can be more deliberate in creating a game plan to improve things.

To optimize this activity:

1. Take this copy of the Assess Your Marriage tool AFTER reading *"Baggage Claim"* and working through the activities and tools embedded in each chapter.
2. Compare the Pre version of this tool to the Post version immediately after reading the book.
3. Complete and compare another Post version at the three-month, six-month, and 12-month marks so you can see how much your thinking has changed and how far your relationship has progressed.

Activity #10
Post – Assess Your Marriage
Rate each category on a scale of 1-10 (10 the greatest 1 the lowest).
Provide a brief reason for the score.

Category	Score	Reason
Goals / Drive/ Aspirations *(Is there a sense that there is a common target or mission that you are accomplishing together?)*		
Sex & Intimacy *(How compatible are your sex drives, definitions of intimacy and priority levels when it comes to sex and intimacy?)*		
Parenting/ Family Values *(Consider whether your similarities and differences around family values and parenting complement each other or clash. Are they effective or damaging?)*		
Dealing with Conflict *(Consider how you resolve conflict in your marriage. Do you feel you have a good understanding of how and when to address issue in your relationship?)*		
Career & Money *(How compatible are you in your style of handling money and prioritizing career?)*		

Household Responsibilities
(Are you happy with your household responsibilities?)

Communication
(Do you feel like you try your best to understand each other's views, feelings, and opinions?)

Faith / Spirituality / Beliefs
(How spiritually compatible are you? Do you assist in each's spiritual growth?)

Friendship with Each Other
(Is your spouse your best friend?)

Managing External Friendships
(Are external relationships prioritized such that they are a help and not a hinderance to your marriage?)

Add the scores for each category to calculate your **Total Score**

Divide the Total Score by 10 to calculate the Average Score of Your Marriage. *(Total Score /10)*

11

Conclusion

In conclusion, the journey through this marriage workbook has been a transformative exploration of self-discovery and relational growth. Through ten purposeful activities, we've delved into the depths of our past social, emotional, and behavioral baggage, unveiling layers of understanding and healing. The exercises have served as catalysts for uncovering untapped communication strategies, nurturing empathy, and fostering a deeper connection within our marriage. By unpacking the baggage that once weighed us down and learning new communication approaches, we've laid the groundwork for a more harmonious, compassionate, and productive relationship.

This workbook isn't just a culmination; it marks the beginning of an ongoing journey towards a richer, more fulfilling partnership built on trust, understanding, and mutual respect. As we continue this journey together, may the insights gained and lessons learned serve as guiding beacons, illuminating our path toward a stronger and more enriching marital bond.

We challenge you to revisit these ten activities as often as they are needed. Keep in mind that even when things are going well, they can always be better. That is part of what makes marriage such an amazing experience. It is the only institution on earth designed for two people to embark upon a journey in which they deliberately work to tame their individual selves and merge into one (*Genesis 2:24; Matthew 19:5... For this reason a man shall leave his father and his mother, and be joined to his wife; and they shall become one flesh.*).

Remember, marriage is not always easy, but it is as simple as providing for, investing in, and empowering one another.... After all, you are a team.

Kimberly H. Miller is a life-learner who is excited about the move of God in this season. She is a simplistic person who sees abundant life as a state of being and not a tangible measurement. Kim believes that each day is a school of change, and she sits in the classroom on the front row, watching God orchestrate and listening to the message of direction. She believes that God wrote the purpose of our lives in our hearts, but life's clutter has blocked area's that we must search deeply to recover. Kimberly believes that this search is her calling to help God's people discover the hidden treasures in their hearts. She has lived out that purpose by mentoring and motivating countless young people, parents, and families through the schools, and the churches and community-based organization to which she has partnered. Kim's favorite saying is... "Walk in Godfidence!"

Dr. Newton H. Miller II has committed over 25 years of his life to the education arena by serving as a middle school and high school mathematics and science teacher, a principal of both middle and high schools and a education professor and associate dean om the university level. He received his doctorate degree in education leadership, which gave him extensive training in successfully developing and coordinating plans for change. Since Newton is a gifted motivator and encourager, he offers a most effective opportunity for you to create your plan to have a great and lasting marriage. Newton's passion is to help others visualize and activate themselves to call forth their own potential to fulfill their purpose in life. Thus, his mantra and ulterior motive is always to educate, motivate, and help them grow.

After facing many challenges, roadblocks, and self-dug pitfalls which he had to conquer and overcome in his own life, Newton has dedicated his research and professional practices to finding what works in educating non-traditional and at-potential populations beginning with strong and healthy families cultures.Newton has been a long-time advocate and supporter of strong families and marriages. He has worked to use education to reverse the cycles of perpetuated dysfunction by dismantling and rebuilding a healthy culture around home - school - community relations. Evidenced in his book, "Why Some Seeds Don't Grow". Throughout the years, he has been active in local ministries focusing on educating and empowering young people (young men in particular) by encouraging and supporting educational attainment, emphasizing vision, purpose, and self-esteem, and healthy marriage relationships. Newton's favorite saying is... "Stay Anxious to Make a Difference!"

For a complete list of our titles and to request signed copies of this book and other titles written by Kim and Dr. Newt visit us at www.newEDproducts.net

Marriage Books

Marriage Simple as P.I.E. - *Baggage Claim*
Kimberly & Dr. Newton Miller II

Kimberly and Newton are very transparent as they share experiences from their own marriage to provide examples that help readers not only see the importance of unpacking the baggage of the past to maintain a healthy relationship, but how to walk through the unpacking process.

Parenting/Mentoring

Why Some Seeds Don't Grow
Dr. Newton Miller

Why Some Seeds Don't Grow, explores ten principles that will help those who mentor, parent, and educate urban youth develop the mindset needed to help those seeds grow, maximize their potential, and accomplish their purpose.

Author Instructor Course

The Published Author: The instructor Course
Kimberly Miller

Step-by-step instructor course for writing and publishing your own book.

Spiritual Seasons Journal Series

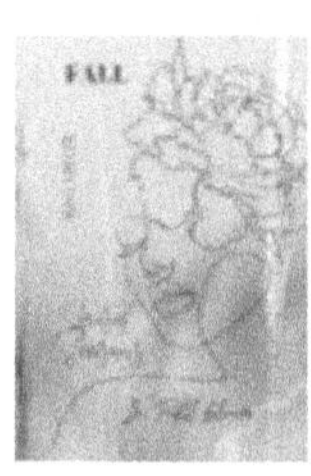

Spiritual Seasons Journal: Fall
Kimberly Miller

Fall is the "letting go to grow season." Fall is unique; everything changes, including the colors of your world. Take time to journal as you watch yourself grow beyond your understanding because when we enter into the season of Fall, we will see ourselves fully bloom in due season.

Spiritual Seasons Journal: Spring
Kimberly Miller

Spring is the season that everything leaps into action. It's the season to maintain and manage the crop. Take time to journal as you watch yourself grow beyond your understanding because when we enter into the season of Spring, we will see ourselves fully bloom in due season.

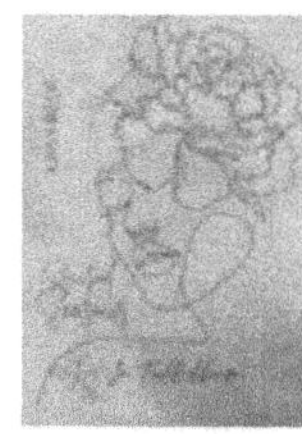

Spiritual Seasons Journal: Winter
Kimberly Miller

Winter is the winning season. This season you will need to prepare for great growth under the surface and take time to journal as you watch yourself grow beyond your understanding. Don't be fooled by cold or dark days in your Winter because there is a win in Winter.

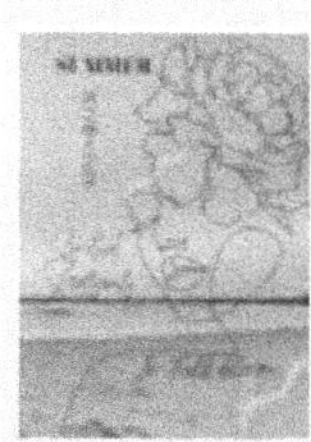

Spiritual Seasons Journal: Summer
Kimberly Miller

Summer is the season of strength. This season, you will need to be ready for all the growth occurring around and in you. Take time to journal as you watch yourself grow beyond your understanding. Because when we understand the seasons of our lives, we will fully bloom in due season.

Children's Books & Activities

Candy Kenya
Kimberly Miller

Candy Kenya presents an easy way to teach children the importance of making good choices and following directions. Children will be reminded of the love that Mommy & Daddy have for them even when it seems like they're just being bossy!

Little Cub
Kimberly Miller

Kids love animals, and learning about them is always fun. This cute little book about Brown bear cubs will help children learn interesting facts about the brown bear. Students will also complete fun activities that support the topic. As a teacher, another way to enjoy this activity book is to copy the activity sheets and coloring pages for students to color, write and discuss. Target ages 0-6

The Potential in You
Kimberly Miller

Teaching children that they have potential and the ability to achieve great things! Target age 1-6

Whoo's Owl
Kimberly Mille

r

Kids love animals, and learning about them is always fun. This cute little book about Owls will help children learn interesting facts about the adorable Owl animal. Students will also complete fun activities that support mastery of the topic. As a teacher, another way to enjoy this activity book is to copy the activity sheets and coloring pages for students to color and discuss. Target ages 0-6

**Launch Kids Forgiveness &
Repentance Sunday School Series**
Kimberly Miller

In this series, children will learn that God's definition of forgiveness means to pardon or excuse; no longer blame or be angry with someone who has done something wrong. Children will also understand that repentance means to turn away from sin, be sorry for your choices, and make new positive choices.

Who Made it ALL?
Kimberly Miller

Children will see the beauty and complexity of the world while learning about landforms, clouds, and volcanoes. They will also understand and acknowledge that someone greater than themselves created everything.

My Little Hands:
Kimberly Miller

Mi'Kayla is a happy little girl, learning that it takes time to grow. She uses her imagination and heart to touch things that she physically can't reach. In this cute little picture book, students will use their imagination to touch the world. They will also gain an understanding of the contractions used in the story.

Animalbet'z Letter A Animals
Kimberly Miller

Kids love animals, and learning about them is always fun. This cute little Animalbet'z book begins with the letter A, animals. Children will learn interesting facts about adorable animals and complete fun activities that support mastery of the topic. Another way to enjoy this activity book is to copy the activity sheets and coloring pages for kids to color. Target age 1st-5th grade

When Cheerleaders Go on STRIKE!
Kimberly Miller

Children love sports and fun activities, but sometimes those activities are measured against others and minimized for what seems popular. In this funny book, learn how Akai, her cheerleading friends, and Coach Jones teach the football team a valuable lesson about the importance of cheerleaders. Target age 3rd-5th grade

Growing in Circles
Kimberly Miller

Shapes make up many things in our world, and circles are one of the most used shapes. A circle is a curved line that meets at the being of the curve. Circles have no breaks or openings, and it is used to make many cool designs, complete other 3D shapes, and for many of the things you use in your home. Check out all the cool ways that you and I are growing in circles.

Dude Journals
Kimberly Miller

This journal is a guide to help us set goals, declare affirmations, and remind us of our importance and value in the world. When we understand who we are, they will show up in the world as strong, purposeful leaders. I'm Troy, and I'm Zion from Ommy'z World Kids, and it's time to journal about your future.

Teen Journal
Kimberly Miller

Growing up can be challenging. Teenagers deal with puberty and all kinds of physical changes. When puberty knocks on our door, life feels a little more difficult and confusing than usual. We, Teens, need a tool to help us express our feelings and deal with our emotions. So spending time journaling can be a positive outlet to reflect upon our daily experiences. This journal is a guide that will help kids set goals, declare affirmations, and remind us of our importance and value. And most importantly, get us on the path to self-discovery. I'm Jada, and I'm Kimani from Ommy'z World Kids, and it's time to journal about your future.

Tory Too Little
Kimberly Miller

This adorable picture book about Tory presents an easy way to teach children the importance of kindness. Children learn that patience and love are keys to growing up and establishing great friendships!

Jayanni's Letter
Kimberly Miller

Jayanni's Letter is a sweet fictional story about a little girl and the loving relationship between her and her grandmother, Abuela. Each day Jayanni reads a beautiful letter from her grandmother that reassures how much she is loved. However, overtime Jayanni is forced to deal with the unfortunate loss of her Abuela. Thankfully Jayanni had special memories of the letters of love written by her Abuela/grandmother that helped her get through her grief and eventually turn the painful situation into a tradition of letter writing.

Zion Lion King of the Jungle
Kimberly Miller

Zion the Lion is a Realistic-Fiction text about a lion who protects the Pride. Zion is a proud Lion who knows the importance of defending and protecting his family and the Jungle that he maintains. Students will enjoy reading the adventures of Zion while learning essential facts about lions. At the end of the story, you will find Lion facts and activities for students to enjoy and educators to implement in the classroom.

Made to Be King
Kimberly Miller

Newt and his dad travel to the Zoo to learn about Elephants. Newt learns that Elephants are the largest land Mammal, and he believes that the Elephant should be King of the Jungle! While talking to the Elephants, Newt realizes that the Elephant, like humans, can be afraid to face their fears.

Kimya the Hyena Hunter
Kimberly Miller

Kimya, the Hyena Hunter, is a Non-Fictional text told by a fictional character. Kimya takes you on a safari adventure to the heights of mountains, the terrain of forest, the fields of grasslands, and the sands of deserts to find the unique mammal the Spotted Hyena.
So come along and grab your hat, camera, and canteen and, most importantly, your imagination, and let's take an inquisitive journey from continent to continent and learn more about the Spotted Hyena.

That's Why I Dance: Layla's Praise
Kimberly Miller

That's Why I Dance: Layla's Praise is about a brilliant and energetic little girl with a vivid imagination who loves to worship through dance. Read how Layla expresses her heart through liturgical dance while inspiring the reader to work hard at achieving their dreams.

To compliment this workbook, get your copy of
Baggage Claim: Provide, Invest & Empower: Covenant Ingredients to Marriage
2nd Edition

www.newEDproducts.net/shop

Inquire about our customized marriage seminars or marriage information sessions (in-person or virtual) where we build a program to meet your specific needs. Contact us at directly: msap@drnewt2.com